W9-AVA-723

HISTORY'S GREATEST DISASTERS

THE SINKING OF THE TITANIC

by Anita Yasuda

Content Consultant
Captain Charles Weeks
Professor Emeritus in Marine Transportation
Maine Maritime Academy

CORE
LIBRARY

Published by ABDO Publishing Company, PO Box 398166, Minneapolis, MN 55439. Copyright © 2014 by Abdo Consulting Group, Inc. International copyrights reserved in all countries. No part of this book may be reproduced in any form without written permission from the publisher. The Core Library™ is a trademark and logo of ABDO Publishing Company.

Printed in the United States of America,
North Mankato, Minnesota
042013
112013
♻ THIS BOOK CONTAINS AT LEAST 10% RECYCLED MATERIALS.

Editor: Jenna Gleisner
Series Designer: Becky Daum

Library of Congress Control Number: 2013932005

Cataloging-in-Publication Data
Yasuda, Anita.
 The sinking of the Titanic / Anita Yasuda.
   p. cm. -- (History's greatest disasters)
ISBN 978-1-61783-960-3 (lib. bdg.)
ISBN 978-1-62403-025-3 (pbk.)
Includes bibliographical references and index.
1. Titanic (Steamship)--Juvenile literature. 2. Shipwrecks--North Atlantic Ocean--Juvenile literature.   I. Title.
910.91634--dc23
                                        2013932005

CONTENTS

CHAPTER ONE

THE ULTIMATE SHIP

Ship No. 401 made news even before work began on it. The White Star Line's new ship would be the largest ship ever built at the time. Millions of dollars were spent building the ship in Belfast, Ireland. The ship would be 883 feet (269 m) long and 92 feet (28 m) wide when it was finished. It would be as tall as an 11-story building.

Newspapers called Titanic a "monster."

In 1908 the White Star Line chose a name that would reflect the ship's huge size: *Titanic*. The ship would be called the RMS *Titanic*. RMS stood for Royal Mail Ship. In addition to carrying passengers, the ship would carry mail and cargo. The *Titanic* would become one of the most famous ships in history but not for the reasons the ship's builders expected.

The Unsinkable Ship

Three thousand men worked for three years to build the *Titanic*. The ship had the best technology of its day. Huge bulkheads divided the ship's hull, or body, into 16 sections. The watertight bulkheads between each section prevented flooding in case of an accident.

Builders stand next to Titanic's giant propellers in Belfast, Ireland, before the ship leaves on its voyage.

A switch on the bridge, where the captain and officers guided the ship, controlled the doors. Even if the first four sections flooded, the *Titanic* would float. Safety features such as these caused the magazine *Shipbuilder* to call the *Titanic* "practically unsinkable."

Captain Smith, *right*, stands with Lord Pirrie, *left*, who oversaw the construction of the *Titanic*.

Titanic's Captain

The *Titanic*'s captain was Edward J. Smith. At the age of 62, Captain Smith had years of sea experience. Wealthy passengers found him charming. They liked to sail on ships he was in charge of. This earned Captain Smith the nickname of "Millionaires' Captain." He commanded many ships on their maiden voyages.

The Maiden Voyage

On April 10, 1912, the *Titanic* left Southampton, England, for New York. There were 2,228 people aboard. Of these, 910 were crew members. Passengers on the *Titanic* were divided into first, second, and third class.

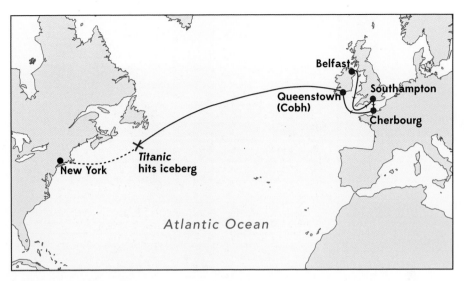

Titanic's Voyage

After leaving Belfast, where it was built, the *Titanic* picked up passengers and cargo in England, France, and Ireland. This map traces the *Titanic*'s voyage. Look at the map and think about the journey people undertook when they immigrated to the United States. Write 200 words describing what you think an emigrant's days on the *Titanic* were like.

Third class was made up of mostly emigrants. These people had scraped together enough money to begin a new life in the United States. But for some of these people, their dreams of living in a new land would never be fulfilled.

On April 15, 1912, the *Titanic* lay at the bottom of the Atlantic Ocean. More than 1,500 people died in the disaster. The world was left to wonder how the unsinkable ship could sink.

CHAPTER TWO

PREPARING FOR VOYAGE

On April 2, 1912, the British Board of Trade (BOT) inspected the *Titanic*. The BOT had to make sure the ship worked well enough to travel. BOT safety rules had not been updated since 1896. These rules said the number of lifeboats needed depended on the ship's tonnage, or amount of space aboard, instead of the number of passengers. According to this rule, the *Titanic* only needed to have 16 lifeboats.

Crew members carry passengers' luggage aboard the Titanic.

The ship's large boat deck could have fit 48 wooden lifeboats. But the ship's designers wanted the deck to look larger, so they only equipped the deck with 16 wooden lifeboats and 4 smaller, collapsible lifeboats. This was enough for BOT safety standards.

Inspectors looked over the *Titanic*'s 16 wooden lifeboats and 4 collapsible lifeboats. They could only hold half of the passengers and crew on the *Titanic*. But this was four more lifeboats than the safety rules required. The BOT decided the *Titanic* was seaworthy.

Electricity Marvel

More than 200 miles (322 km) of cable delivered electricity to every room on the *Titanic*. Electricity ran everything from the 4 elevators to the 10,000 lights. The *Titanic*'s steam generators produced more electricity than many electrical plants on land at the time.

A Sight to See

For seven days, crowds came to see the *Titanic* in Southampton. It was breathtaking. No one could help but be amazed. It rose six decks high. It had four massive funnels that towered above the deck. The

Each gigantic funnel rose 62 feet (19 m) high, adding to the ship's enormous appearance.

steam and smoke from the 6,000 tons (5,443 metric tons) of coal needed to keep the 29 boilers and 159 furnaces going escaped from only three funnels. The fourth funnel was only there to make the ship look grander.

The final preparations for the *Titanic's* voyage began on April 10, 1912. First a short lifeboat drill was held. Sailors rowed two lifeboats around to make sure they worked. The rest of the *Titanic's* crew, including stewards, carpenters, and florists, hurried to make sure everything was in order. Cranes brought in cargo of books, glassware, and food. Food cargo included 75,000 pounds (34,019 kg) of fresh meat, 35,000 fresh eggs, and 1,750 quarts (1,927 L) of ice cream. The kitchen staff would need these supplies to prepare 6,000 meals a day.

Wealthy Passengers

The *Titanic's* voyage attracted many wealthy and powerful people. President William Howard Taft's aide Major Archibald Butt was aboard. Isidor Straus, a co-owner of Macy's department store, and his wife Ida were also on the ship. But the richest man on the *Titanic* was businessman John Jacob Astor IV. Astor was one of the wealthiest men in the world at the time.

Boarding Begins

Passengers began arriving on the morning of April 10, 1912. Many first-class passengers traveled with

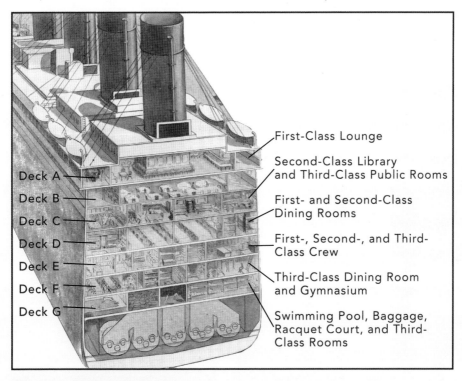

First-Class Lounge

Second-Class Library
and Third-Class Public Rooms

First- and Second-Class
Dining Rooms

First-, Second-, and Third-
Class Crew

Third-Class Dining Room
and Gymnasium

Swimming Pool, Baggage,
Racquet Court, and Third-
Class Rooms

Deck A
Deck B
Deck C
Deck D
Deck E
Deck F
Deck G

Titanic Cross Section

This diagram shows a cross section of the *Titanic*. After
reading about the building and preparing of the *Titanic*,
what do you imagine the interior of the ship looked like?
How would you design it differently?

servants, pets, and lots of luggage. One wealthy

passenger brought 14 trunks, 4 suitcases, and 4 crates

filled with necklaces, gowns, and furs. A first-class

ticket for the *Titanic* cost $2,500. Today that would be

about $57,200. At noon three whistles signaled the

Titanic's departure. It took seven tugboats to tow the

ship away from the dock.

CHAPTER THREE

LIFE ABOARD

Over the next four days, passengers settled in to enjoy the voyage. First-class rooms were very luxurious. They had many modern comforts, including telephones. If there was anything a first-class passenger wanted, he or she only had to ring a call bell. A cabin steward would come right away. Two parlor suites on Deck B were the most expensive. Today they would cost more than $100,000. The suites

This re-creation depicts Titanic's Grand Staircase, which was designed for first-class passengers to use.

had their own private promenade.

The *Titanic*'s second-class rooms were equal to first-class rooms on other ships. Even the *Titanic*'s third-class area was nicer than most ships. Third-class rooms had heat and running water. The majority of cabins had berths for four to six passengers.

Wonders of the Titanic

The *Titanic* was like a floating town. It had two libraries and several fine restaurants. The ship had exercise rooms, a squash court, and decks lit by electric lamps for walking and playing games on. First-class passengers could relax in the Turkish baths for

A man exercises on a rowing machine in the first-class gymnasium.

only one dollar. But the nicest luxury on the *Titanic* was the heated swimming pool.

Guests spent much of their time socializing. First- and second-class ladies read or played cards. Men met in the smoking room. Passengers could also listen to and request songs from the *Titanic's* two bands. Musician bandmaster Wallace Hartley learned all 352 tunes in the White Star Line music book by heart.

Dinnertime

The song "The Roast Beef of Old England" let first- and second-class passengers know when lunch or dinner was being served. The *Titanic* had six different dining rooms and cafés. Revolving doors led to the elegant first-class dining room. Here passengers feasted on ten-course meals. Second-class passengers were treated to six-course meals. The second-class dining room had large swivel chairs.

Third-class passengers also enjoyed hearty meals. Compared to other passenger ships, the third class had nice public spaces. The two third-class dining rooms had family-style tables and portals to let in sunlight.

Radio Telegraph Messages

Passengers loved sending telegraph messages to loved ones with the ship's wireless telegraph. It was a great novelty of the time. They kept wireless operators Jack Phillips and Harold Bride very busy. Passengers paid approximately $36 in today's money to send a ten-word message.

Colonel Archibald Gracie survived the sinking of the *Titanic*. His book *The Truth about the Titanic* became a famous story of the disaster. In it he writes about what he did on the ship:

> *On the first days of the voyage . . . I had devoted my time to social enjoyment and to the reading of books taken from the ship's well-supplied library. I enjoyed myself as if I were in a summer palace on the seashore, surrounded with every comfort. . . . But when Sunday morning came, I considered it high time to begin my customary exercises, and determined for the rest of the voyage to patronize the squash racquet court, the gymnasium, the swimming pool, etc.*

> Source: Colonel Archibald Gracie. The Truth about the *Titanic*. New York: Mitchell Kennerley, 1913. Print. 5.

Consider Your Audience

Review the passage, and think about how you would change it for a different audience, such as your friends. Write a postcard, giving the same information for the new audience. How does your writing differ from the author's original text and why?

CHAPTER FOUR

ICE SIGHTED

On Sunday morning, April 14, 1912, passengers woke up to sunny skies. They enjoyed breakfast, and some attended the Sunday church service. A lifeboat drill was scheduled for that morning. All ships of the White Star Line had to have Sunday lifeboat drills. The drills were meant to prepare the passengers and crew in case of an emergency. But on this Sunday,

This illustration of Titanic colliding with an iceberg appeared on the front page of the Sphere, a London newspaper, on April, 20, 1912.

The area of the Atlantic Ocean where *Titanic* sank was covered with ice chunks.

Captain Smith canceled the *Titanic*'s drill. No reason was ever given.

Ice Warnings

At 9:00 a.m. the *Titanic* began receiving messages that warned of icebergs and ice fields. Captain Smith changed the *Titanic*'s course a bit south, but he kept the ship's speed the same. More warnings came later in the day. There was no direct telegraph line to the bridge. Radio operators Jack Phillips and Harold Bride had to hand-deliver messages to Captain Smith and the officers.

At 11:00 p.m. Phillips was busy sending passengers' telegrams. A message from a nearby ship, the *Californian*, came in. The *Californian* reported it was surrounded by ice and had stopped for the night, suggesting *Titanic* should do the same. Phillips told the *Californian's* operator to leave him alone because he was working. The *Californian's* operator turned off his system and went to bed.

Missed Distress Calls

Ten minutes after the *Californian's* operator turned off the ship's wireless, the *Titanic* hit an iceberg. The *Californian* never received any of the *Titanic's* distress calls. After the *Titanic* disaster, the Radio Act was passed. This act required wireless systems to be operated 24 hours a day.

Jack Phillips, the senior wireless operator of the *Titanic*, did not survive the sinking.

Iceberg Sighted

Above deck, two lookouts, Frederick Fleet and Reginald Lee, stood on a high perch called the crow's nest. They peered into the darkness. The lookout before them had told them to watch out for low pieces of ice. Fleet and Lee had no binoculars. Their only source of light came from the stars.

Suddenly at 11:40 p.m., Fleet saw a large shape directly in front of the *Titanic*. It was an iceberg. He quickly rang the crow's nest bell and phoned the bridge to warn the officers and Captain Smith. Officers changed the ship's direction. But it was too late.

The Unthinkable

The iceberg had scraped the starboard, or right, side of the *Titanic*. Seawater started to rush in. Captain Smith and the *Titanic*'s designer, Thomas Andrews Jr., checked the damage. The first 5 of the *Titanic*'s 16 sections were split open. The hull was not watertight. Andrews told Captain Smith the unthinkable: the *Titanic* was sinking.

Icebergs

An iceberg can be as small as a car or as big as a town. Approximately 90 percent of an iceberg is below the water's surface. The underwater part of the iceberg is the most dangerous to ships because it cannot be seen.

The situation was desperate. Captain Smith ordered Phillips to send out a distress call at 12:15 a.m. Phillips sent the international distress signal over and over again. Later he added SOS to his messages. SOS is a code that radio operators can send to call for help.

Chunks of Ice

Many passengers barely noticed the collision. Some passengers discovered ice on the deck and began playing with it. Most passengers did not know they were in danger until stewards knocked on their doors to warn them.

In the *Sphere*, *Titanic* survivor Lawrence Beesley wrote about his first reaction to the disaster:

> I felt a slight jar. Then soon afterwards there was a second shock, but it was not sufficiently large to cause any anxiety. . . . At first I thought that the ship had lost a propeller. I went up on deck in my dressing gown and I found only a few people there. They had noticed . . . a huge iceberg go by close to the side of the boat. They thought that we had just grazed it. None of us of course had any conception that she had been pierced below by part of a submerged iceberg. . . . Without any thought of disaster I retired to my cabin to read until we started again.

Source: Lawrence Beesley. "The Wreck of the 'Titanic.'" The Sphere, April 27, 1912. Print. 68.

Nice View

Compare the reactions of passenger Beesley and operator Phillips. What do the two reactions tell you about how the crew and the passengers viewed the accident differently? Write a short essay comparing the two points of view.

CHAPTER FIVE

A SHIP IN DISTRESS

At 12:25 a.m. Captain Smith ordered the crew to start filling the lifeboats. He ordered crew members to board women and children first. The *Titanic*'s crew worked hard to fill the lifeboats, but they were disorganized. Some officers thought the boats would buckle if they were filled with too many people. The first lifeboat lowered was less than half full. The crew continued lowering half-empty lifeboats

Because there were not enough lifeboats to fit all passengers, only women and children were allowed to board the first lifeboats.

into the water. As the *Titanic*'s bow sank deeper, passengers realized they were going to be left on the ship. Many of them panicked to get onto a lifeboat.

Call for Help

By 1:00 a.m. the crew began sending off distress rockets. They could see a ship in the distance. It is believed the ship was the *Californian*, but the ship did not respond. Captain Arthur Rostron of the *Carpathia* was approximately 58 miles (93 km) away when he heard the *Titanic*'s distress signals. He raced the *Carpathia* toward the *Titanic*.

The Survivors

By 2:20 a.m. the *Titanic* was completely underwater. In less than three hours, the unsinkable ship had sunk. Passengers left aboard

Devoted Musicians

During the evacuation, bandmaster Wallace Hartley gathered all the musicians together. They played songs to keep the frightened passengers' spirits up right until the ship sank. None of the *Titanic*'s musicians survived.

Harold Bride, center, survived the sinking of the Titanic with severely frozen feet.

jumped into the icy Atlantic Ocean. Others were pulled down with the *Titanic*. A few fought to get on an upside-down lifeboat that was never launched. Wireless operator Harold Bride and others stood on top of the lifeboat all night. Bride survived.

Lifeboat passengers listened to the swimmers' screams as they cried out for help for an entire hour. Only one lifeboat went back to rescue them. Survivors

More First-Class Survivors

Almost all first-class women and children survived. But approximately only half of the third-class women survived. Less than one in three third-class children survived. One reason for this was that third-class passengers did not have direct access to the boat deck, where lifeboats were located.

feared swimmers would swamp their boats. They also thought suction from the *Titanic* might pull them down.

The Rescue

In the early morning, survivors saw the hull of a ship steaming toward them. The *Carpathia* arrived just after 4:00 a.m. It picked up any survivors it could find and steamed toward the United States. The *Carpathia* reached New York with 712 *Titanic* survivors on April 18, 1912.

The public waited for news of the *Titanic*. At first it was believed everyone aboard was fine. Slowly the truth came over the wires. The famous *Titanic* had struck an iceberg and sank. More than 1,500 people were killed.

A group of *Titanic* survivors talk while aboard the *Carpathia*.

EXPLORE ONLINE

Newspapers rushed to print stories of the *Titanic* disaster. Most of the stories had false information. Read the passage on the Web site below. Compare it to what you learned in Chapter Five. How do you think this disaster would be covered today? Write four headlines telling the truth about the disaster. How do your headlines compare to those on the Web site?

Titanic **in the News**
www.mycorelibrary.com/titanic

CHAPTER SIX

THE *TITANIC'S* LEGACY

For 75 years, the *Titanic*'s location in the Atlantic Ocean was a mystery. Then on September 1, 1985, ocean explorer Dr. Robert Ballard and his team found the ship. After days of looking at pictures of the seafloor, a piece of the *Titanic* flashed across the team's screen.

The team used an underwater vehicle named *Alvin* to film the *Titanic*. It sent back amazing video.

Titanic's hull rests 12,500 feet (3,810 m) below the surface on the Atlantic Ocean's floor.

A smaller robot called *Jason Jr.* explored areas of the ship *Alvin* could not. *Jason Jr.* went past the officers' area. A sign saying "Authorized Personnel Only" was still visible. Later dives showed that the iceberg did not rip the ship open. Instead the iceberg opened the *Titanic*'s seams to approximately the size of a door. This led to the ship splitting in two.

The Big Piece

Today only the company RMS Titanic Inc. can retrieve objects from the *Titanic*. The US government gave RMS Titanic Inc. this permission in 1987. More than 6,000 artifacts have been recovered. One of the artifacts is a piece of the *Titanic*'s hull. Called the Big Piece, it weighs about 15 tons (14 metric tons) and

Alvin tours the remaining deck of the Titanic in 1986.

is more than 26 feet (8 m) long. Not everyone thinks taking artifacts from the *Titanic* is a good idea. Some people view the *Titanic* as a grave. They do not want anything taken from the ship.

The Fascination Lives On

Many teams have visited the *Titanic* since 1985. Filmmaker James Cameron has made 33 dives down to the *Titanic*. His tiny robot *Gilligan* went through the

Titanic. It sent back many pictures including photos of the wireless room.

The *Titanic*'s voyage ended on April 15, 1912. But more than 100 years after the sinking, interest in the disaster is still strong. Objects from the *Titanic* tour the globe. Tourist submarines visit the site. The *Titanic* will always be remembered as the luxurious, unsinkable ship that sank. Those who died in the disaster will be remembered forever.

Artifacts

Musical instruments and toys are some of the 6,000 items salvaged from the *Titanic*. One passenger, Adolphe Saalfeld, planned on selling his perfume to stores in New York. He survived the sinking, but his perfume was left behind. Saalfeld brought 65 bottles of perfume onto the *Titanic*, and 62 of them have been recovered from the wreck.

This chronometer, a clock used to navigate longitude, is one of the many artifacts found among the *Titanic* wreckage.

FURTHER EVIDENCE

There is a lot of information about the *Titanic*'s legacy in Chapter Six. What is the main point of this chapter? What key evidence supports this point? Visit the Web site below. Take notes as you read the article. Are your notes different from or similar to the information in the chapter?

Lost Liners

www.mycorelibrary.com/titanic

IMPORTANT DATES

1908
The White Star Line names Ship No. 401 the RMS Titanic.

Apr. 2
The Titanic passes its safety inspection and departs from Belfast, Ireland, for Southampton, England.

Apr. 10
The Titanic leaves Southampton, England, for New York on its maiden voyage.

1912

Apr. 15
At 1:00 a.m. Titanic crew members begin setting off distress rockets.

Apr. 15
At 2:20 a.m. the Titanic sinks with more than 1,500 lives lost.

Apr. 15
Shortly after 4:00 a.m. the Carpathia arrives and rescues 712 Titanic passengers.

1912

Apr. 14

The *Titanic's* starboard side strikes an iceberg.

Apr. 15

The *Titanic* sends out a distress call at 12:15 a.m., which the *Carpathia* responds to.

Apr. 15

At 12:25 a.m. Captain Smith orders the lifeboats be filled with women and children first.

Apr. 18

The *Carpathia* arrives in New York with survivors from the *Titanic*.

1985

A French and US research team discovers the sunken *Titanic* on September 1.

2012

The *Titanic* disaster observes its one hundredth anniversary on April 15.

Why Do I Care?

The *Titanic* disaster happened more than 100 years ago. But accidents still happen at sea. What technology do modern ships have to help them avoid disasters? What safety regulations are in place that might not exist without the *Titanic*? Think about training, lifeboats, and communication between ships.

You Are There

This book discusses the lack of lifeboats on the *Titanic*. Imagine you are traveling on the *Titanic* to your new home in the United States. You have been told to get into a lifeboat, but there is no room for your family. How do you feel about evacuating the ship? Be sure to include which class you are traveling in.

Say What?

Reading about the *Titanic* can mean learning a lot of new vocabulary. Find five words in this book that you have never seen or heard before. Use a dictionary to find out what they mean. Then rewrite the meanings in your own words. Use each word in a sentence.

Surprise Me

This book discusses the *Titanic's* number of lifeboats. Which facts about the *Titanic's* lifeboats did you find most surprising? Write a few sentences about each fact. Why did you find them surprising?

GLOSSARY

berth
a single bed on a ship

bow
the front end of a ship

bridge
an elevated part of a ship where the captain and officers guide the ship

bulkhead
a structure built between compartments to keep water from reaching other areas

emigrant
a person leaving his or her country to settle in another

hull
the body of a ship

luxury
expensive and nice but unnecessary

maiden voyage
a ship's first voyage, or trip

promenade
an area to walk along

seaworthy
safe for a sea voyage

squash
an indoor game played with racquets and a ball on a court

steward
an employee of the ship who serves passengers

wireless telegraph
a form of radio communication popular in the early 1900s

LEARN MORE

Books

Adams, Simon. *Titanic*. New York: DK Publishing, 2009.

Brown, Don. *All Stations! Distress! April 15, 1912: The Day the Titanic Sank.* New York: Flash Point, 2008.

Carson, Mary Kay. *What Sank the World's Biggest Ship?* New York: Sterling Publishing, 2012.

Web Links

To learn more about the sinking of the *Titanic*, visit ABDO Publishing Company online at **www.abdopublishing.com**. Web sites about the sinking of the *Titanic* are featured on our Book Links page. These links are routinely monitored and updated to provide the most current information available. Visit **www.mycorelibrary.com** for free additional tools for teachers and students.

INDEX

ABOUT THE AUTHOR

Anita Yasuda is the author of more than 60 books for children. She enjoys writing biographies, chapter books, and books about science and social studies. Anita lives with her family and her dog in Huntington Beach, California.